Original title:
Sweetgrass Sonnets

Copyright © 2025 Creative Arts Management OÜ
All rights reserved.

Author: Julian Carmichael
ISBN HARDBACK: 978-1-80567-001-8
ISBN PAPERBACK: 978-1-80567-081-0

Whispers Beneath the Canopy

In the forest, laughter swells,
As squirrels tell their cheeky tales.
With acorn hats and tiny coats,
They dance beneath the leafy vaults.

A bird with flair tries comedy,
Telling jokes to a puzzled bee.
The trees chuckle in the breeze,
Rustling leaves with gentle tease.

A rabbit hops, a playful sight,
Chasing shadows left and right.
The sun peeks through with a giggle,
While flowers sway and sometimes wiggle.

Beneath the canopy, we laugh,
Enjoying nature's silly staff.
Life's a jest among the trees,
Where humor thrives and worries freeze.

The Secrets of Blooming Hollows

In the hollow where flowers bloom,
A gopher sings, dispelling gloom.
His high-pitched voice alarms the bees,
Who buzz around with frantic pleas.

Lilies waltz in the warm sunlight,
While daisies giggle at their height.
A rabbit tries to join the dance,
Ends up tangled, not a chance!

The butterflies paint the air bright,
They flutter by with pure delight.
With secret moves, they spread their cheer,
As petals laugh, 'You're late, my dear!'

Every bloom has a story to share,
Of quiet moments, light as air.
In the hollow's embrace, we find,
Nature's secrets, hilariously kind.

Fragrant Dreams of the Open Sky

In the open fields where aromas play,
A sunflower twirls to greet the day.
With winds so sweet, they tease and flirt,
While daisies giggle in their shirts.

A bumblebee dons a little tux,
Buzzing jokes that get the ducks,
All in line for a comedy show,
With fragrant blooms putting on a glow.

Clouds drift by, wearing funny hats,
As butterflies join in, like acrobats.
They flutter and dance, the sun's warm kiss,
Beneath the bright sky, we dream of bliss.

In these fragrant dreams, we play so sweet,
Life's laughter transpires in every heartbeat.
The open sky brings joy and cheer,
With every petal whispering near.

The Harmony of Seasons

Seasons change with a playful wink,
Spring sneezes, and winter's on the brink.
Summer grins, bringing sunlit glee,
While autumn laughs, 'Look, a red-leaf spree!'

In harmony, they share a song,
With silly notes that all go wrong.
Snowflakes swirl in a frosty jig,
As raindrops dance a tiny gig.

The trees tell tales with branchy hands,
Each season's humor perfectly planned.
A squirrel taunts a shy little mouse,
In the great big theatre of their house.

From sunlit days to snowy nights,
Nature's laughter sparks sheer delights.
The seasons spin their merry dance,
Celebrating life's whimsical chance.

The Spirit of the Pastures

Cows in a row, wearing silly hats,
Chasing their tails, just like acrobats.
The sheep gossip low, munching on grass,
While pigs join the dance, with a waltz, not a hash.

The wind whispers jokes, tickling the trees,
As squirrels throw acorns, beg for some cheese.
Under the sun, all creatures agree,
A day full of laughter, wild and carefree.

Song of the Golden Hour

Bees buzzing tunes, like a band on a spree,
Flowers are swaying, lost in the melody.
The sun winks a gold tooth, setting the scene,
As rabbits wear shades, looking quite keen.

A frog croaks a solo, a slippery star,
While crickets join in from fields near and far.
The dance of the day, under skies painted bright,
With hiccups of laughter, a pure delight.

Fables of the Fields

Once lived a squirrel with quite the tall tale,
Of acorns so big, they could launch a sail.
The hens chimed in with a flapping of wings,
Claiming they'd found the prize of all things.

Mice gathered round, eyes wide with dread,
As the cow spun tales from the barn's cozy bed.
With each twist and turn, giggles arose,
In fields where imagination endlessly grows.

Visions of Verdant Stillness

In a still green nook, where dreams intertwine,
A hedgehog plays chess, sipping on brine.
The trees shake their leaves, adding some flair,
While the grass hums a tune, light as air.

A fox struts by, with a wink so sly,
"I'm the king of the meadow!" he claims with a sigh.
But the daisies just giggle, tossing their heads,
Weaving fun riddles from their leafy beds.

Nature's Resilient Heart

In springtime blooms, the plants conspire,
With leafy wigs that never tire.
A flower wears a goofy grin,
As bees throw dance parties, wild within.

The trees gossip in a rustling spree,
While squirrels plan a shindig with glee.
Roots tickle toes from underground,
Nature's laughter, a joyous sound.

Clouds do the polka, feeling spry,
While worms wear top hats, oh my, oh my!
The daisies clap in rhythmic delight,
As sunlight winks in the fading light.

So here's to Earth, with her wild charm,
A garden party, full of warm.
We'll dance with plants, oh what a start,
In this land of nature's resilient heart.

Footsteps in the Field

Amidst the grasses, a trail runs free,
Where frogs hold meetings on their decree.
With croaks of laughter, they jump and play,
While crickets serenade the end of the day.

Butterflies flit in their bright attire,
Hosting fashion shows never to tire.
Each step we take, they glide and tease,
Whispering secrets in the hum of the breeze.

The field is a canvas, so wild and wide,
With daisies bringing their whimsical pride.
An ant parade marches in lines,
Uniformity in mismatched designs!

So come join the frolic in nature's flow,
Where laughter is plenty and worries all go.
Just follow the footsteps on this merry ride,
In the playful embrace of the countryside.

Dance of the Meadow

In fields so wide, the daisies prance,
The butterflies join the silly dance.
A buzzing bee, with a tiny hat,
Says, "Watch me twirl!" And, oh, how 'bout that?

The rabbits laugh, in their fluffy suits,
While ladybugs wear their best green boots.
A squirrel jumps, thinking he can glide,
But lands in a patch of mud, what a ride!

Grass blades sway with a giggling sound,
As nature's jokes carry all around.
The wildflowers wink in playful glee,
While the wind teases, "Come dance with me!"

So join the fun, let your spirit out,
In this meadow, there's no room for doubt.
Life's a party, with no end in sight,
Laugh with the daisies, 'til the sun's last light.

Litanies of the Land

Ode to the dirt, where the worms do sway,
They groove and wiggle in their own way.
The trees clap leaves, what a raucous crowd,
Whispering secrets, oh so loud!

The hills roll over, giving a chuckle,
As rocks play tag, avoiding the buckle.
The cactus poses, full of sharp pride,
"Just look at me, what a wild ride!"

Clouds gather round, twisting in jest,
Creating shapes, at nature's behest.
A cat on a fence, with a grand sigh,
Says, "I'm the king—just wait for the pie!"

In this land, where nonsense is art,
Each creature plays its colorful part.
The sun sets low, with a wink and cheer,
Promising laughter, year after year.

A Journey Through the Green

Through leafy lanes, where mischief hides,
I stumbled upon some very bold rides.
A toad on a log, with a frog kind of grin,
Said, "Hop on board! Let the fun begin!"

The flowers giggled with colors so bright,
Tickling the breeze with sheer delight.
A gopher popped up to share a quick joke,
"I'm not underground, I'm just a laid-back bloke!"

The creek laughed softly, dancing its way,
As pebbles tried splashing, but missed the play.
A bee buzzed through, wearing a crown,
"Queen of the nectar, don't bring me down!"

So trek through the green, let your spirit roam,
Each twist and turn feels just like home.
With giggles galore, let your worries flee,
In this wild wonder, just be carefree!

Nature's Timekeeper

Tick-tock goes the forest clock,
With squirrels in bowties, it's quite a shock.
A snail on the path plays a slow old tune,
While grasshoppers strut like they own the moon.

The sun peeks in, with a grin so bright,
"I'm nearly here, so get ready for flight!"
The shadows stretch long, like they're taking a nap,
While crickets prepare for an evening rap.

The flowers close up, it's time to rest,
But the daisies argue, "We're still the best!"
A wise old owl clears its throat to speak,
"It's time for the night—don't you dare sneak!"

So follow the rhythm, the heartbeat of trees,
Nature's own dance, carried on the breeze.
Laugh with the stars as they twinkle and play,
In this timeless moment, let joy light your way.

The Embrace of Wildness

In the woods, a squirrel doth chatter,
Scrambling up trees, all grace and splatter.
A raccoon's dance, oh what a sight!
Stealing snacks under the moonlight.

The porcupine's hug is a risky affair,
With quills like needles—beware, beware!
The owl hoots, wise yet a bit absurd,
In the wild, every voice is heard.

Frogs croak a tune that's quite out of tune,
While a skunk ambles by, smelling like ruin.
Yet nature giggles at its own folly,
In the embrace of wildness, oh, so jolly!

Leaves rustle softly, a breezy jest,
Nature's own comic—a spunky fest.
With every laugh, the forest feels bright,
In wildness's arms, we twirl with delight.

Nature Reflects

Mirror ponds, where the ducks take a dive,
Reflecting the chaos of life, we arrive.
The beaver builds houses that sway and float,
As fish pass by in a scaly coat.

Sunflowers grin, turned to the sun,
While ants march on, thinking it's fun.
A wind whispers tales of mischief and glee,
Nature's a circus, just wait and see!

Clouds puff up, like a comic's weird hat,
Drawing laughter from a nearby cat.
Reflection reveals a kooky ballet,
In the wild, every day's a fun play.

So let's join the dance, twirl in the air,
Nature's the stage, strip down your care.
With laughter and joy, our spirits ignite,
In nature's reflection, everything's right.

Fragments of Serenity

A butterfly flutters on a dandelion's fluff,
While a puppy leaps—oh, that's just rough stuff!
In peaceful moments, the laughter can swell,
Nature's own tale, it's a quirky spell.

Dragonflies zip in a whimsical chase,
Buzzing around like they're lost in space.
A turtle's slow waddle brings fitful grins,
Life's simple pleasures, where real fun begins.

Breezes carry whispers of playful delight,
As chirping birds join in a musical fight.
Nature's serenity is broken by cheer,
Fragments of laughter, sown far and near.

In every leaf's rustle, there's humor unseen,
Life in the woods is a lighthearted scene.
So let's savor each grin, each giggle, each play,
In fragments of joy, come what may!

Voices in the Verdure

The trees are chattering, gossiping loud,
As mushrooms pop up, all wearing a shroud.
Squirrels debate on acorns to hoard,
In the verdure's voice, all laughter's restored.

A deer prances by in a dappled dance,
While crickets make music, giving a chance.
Sunlight dapples paths with playful grace,
In the chorus of life, we share this space.

In the bushes, a rabbit conveys a jest,
While raccoons plan parties, oh what a fest!
Voices in verdure, melodious and free,
Nature's a laugh, come sit with me!

With every rustle, a chuckle is found,
In the forest of whimsy, joy knows no bound.
So step lightly here, join the jubilant spree,
In the verdant embrace, we all laugh with glee.

Serenity in Spirals

In the garden, the weeds hold a dance,
With the breeze they twirl, a whimsical chance.
They giggle and sway like they've found a friend,
In a nature's party that never will end.

The bees buzz along with a muddled tune,
While the squirrels perform, they think they're in June.
The daisies wear smiles, all colors in show,
As the sun winks quietly, a grand maestro.

We laugh at the chaos, the ants on parade,
Strutting like models, oh, what a charade!
Nature is chuckling, a sweet, silly jest,
In this spiral of joy, we find our best rest.

With every small whirl, we tumble and spin,
In laughter, we find the world's greatest grin.
So join in this flair, let your spirit unwind,
For in laughter and giggles, true peace you will find.

Echoing Footsteps

Walking through the woods with my shoes untied,
I trip on a root, and I just can't hide.
The birds start to laugh, it's quite the display,
As I tumble and roll, in a comical way.

The trees are my witnesses, they rustle with glee,
As I wear nature's carpet more flat on my knee.
The path is a jester, it twists with delight,
In this echo of folly, I take flight.

Every step in the mud is a splatter of fun,
With a dance of my feet, under the sun.
The mushrooms are cheering, they're rooting me on,
As I put on a show till the daylight is gone.

So, here's to the laughter that nature bestows,
In the wobbly steps, that's how humor grows.
Let's leap on the trails, with joy as our guide,
In the forest of giggles, let's happily slide.

The Veil of Verdure

Beneath the green canopy, mischief takes flight,
Where the leaves play hide-and-seek day and night.
The ferns wear their fronds like a crown on their head,
While the flowers offer tea, freshly brewed and spread.

In the shade of the willows, the rabbits hold court,
With a jest and a nibble, they comedically sort.
They discuss all the gossip that buzzes around,
Oh, the vines have their secrets, they're tightly bound!

As the sun sets the stage, everything gleams,
The critters start acting out wild, wacky dreams.
The grasshoppers croon, while the crickets compose,
In this whimsical tale where the laughter just flows.

So when life gets leafy and tangled and fleet,
Remember the joy of each whimsical beat.
For within nature's magic, the fun won't deter,
In the veil of verdure, our spirits confer.

Tresses of the Wind

The wind has a style all its own, oh so free,
It teases my hair, a wild jubilee.
With each playful gust, my locks take a chance,
As if Mother Nature has started a dance.

I chase after rainbows that flutter and dart,
While the clouds giggle softly, oh what a part!
The tresses of breezes tickle my face,
In this whirlwind of joy, I find my own space.

The flowers all wave, "Take a whirl with us!"
While the sun smiles down, sending laughter and fuss.
Nature's own beauty, a spectacle grand,
In the chaos of joy, let's make our own band.

So, let's spin with the wind, in a frolicsome way,
Laughing at moments that brighten our day.
With the world as our stage and delight in the air,
Embrace the tresses of fun, without a care.

A Melody of the Dusk

The sun winks down, a cheeky glance,
While shadows gather, eager to dance.
Crickets chirp a silly tune,
Beneath the light of a lazy moon.

A squirrel juggles acorns with flair,
While flowers giggle without a care.
The breeze brings whispers, sweet and light,
As evening wraps the day so tight.

Fireflies twinkle, the night's delight,
With glow-in-the-dark jumps in flight.
As laughter weaves through the trees,
Nature sings with playful ease.

So let us bask in this twilight show,
Where joy is simple and laughter flows.
In every rustle, a chuckle's found,
As dusk paints fun all around.

Reflections in Nature's Mirror

A pond reflects a bird with flair,
Trying to balance, unaware of air.
The lily pads giggle, what a sight,
As frogs croak out in sheer delight.

A leaf slides down, a slippery prank,
While turtles chuckle from their bank.
The sunbeams dance on water's face,
As nature puts on a comical grace.

Bees buzz by with their silly drones,
Chewing on blossoms while talking in tones.
A breeze tickles the grass just so,
Causing flowers to giggle and grow.

In this mirror, life takes a turn,
With laughter echoing as we learn.
Reflections tease, with humor to borrow,
Nature's canvas, bright with tomorrow.

Breezes of Endless Wonder

A gust brings whispers of colorful tales,
As dandelions dance like tiny sails.
The wind has jokes that carry far,
Tickling the leaves, a playful star.

Clouds float lazily, shapes of delight,
One looks like a cat, the other a bite.
As sunbeams tickle the fields of green,
Laughter bounces where we've been.

A butterfly flutters, trying to glide,
Mistaken for a truck, with pollen inside.
While mice hold a meeting, plotting their feats,
Squeaking about all the tasty treats.

In every breeze, a chuckle resides,
Nature's humor with nothing to hide.
With every gust, a new story flies,
Bringing smiles beneath the skies.

The Poetry of Growth

Tiny seeds whisper beneath the ground,
Wishing for sunshine, silly and round.
With every sprout, a giggling jest,
As plants poke heads up, seeking the best.

Worms wiggle dance in joyful delight,
Helping the soil make everything right.
A raincloud grumbles, then bursts with glee,
Showering magic 'til roots can't see.

Branches stretch up, reaching for fame,
While pine cones joke, calling their name.
With roots intertwined, they share a laugh,
Growing together, their secret path.

As seasons turn, they bloom and sway,
Nature's comedy in a bright bouquet.
In this grand play, the best part?
Growth keeps us laughing, heart to heart.

The Art of Being

In the dance of life, we twirl and spin,
Juggling jobs and snacks, where to begin?
With socks unmatched, and hair askew,
Being us is an art, and it's never through!

We paint our truths with chocolate sauce,
And laugh at the mess, we're our own boss.
The floors may squeak, the dishes pile high,
But at least we can laugh till we nearly cry!

In the middle of chaos, we find our jam,
Spilling secrets like toddlers and ham.
Who needs perfection, or well-laid plans?
Life's better with sprinkles and crazy fans!

So here's to the quirky, the odd, and the bold,
The mishaps of life that are worth more than gold.
Raise a toast with your cup full of cheer,
To the art of being, oh so dear!

A Garden of Memories

In the patch of our past, weeds take a stand,
Where memories grow wild, unplanned, unplanned.
We planted some laughter, sprinkled with tears,
In our garden of time, surrounded by years.

With sunflowers tall and daisies shy,
We talk to our plants, wondering why.
The carrots won't sprout, the tomatoes just frown,
Yet our love in the soil keeps us from down.

We dig through the dirt for treasures untold,
But find only socks from the neighbors of old.
The butterflies flit, whispering lies,
While we plot our escape with a pie in the sky.

And when the rains come, we dance in the muck,
Wishing for sunshine, but happy with luck.
In a garden of memories, chaotic and bright,
We smile at the weeds that join in the plight.

When the Earth Whispers

When the earth leans down to share a secret,
We listen close, our hearts ready to accept it.
But squirrels are barking, the frogs start to croak,
It's hard to hear wisdom in all that hoax!

The trees gossip softly, their branches sway,
Complaining of walkers who can't find their way.
The rocks roll their eyes as we trip on their toes,
While daisies snicker at our garden woes.

The rivers chuckle, murmuring tales,
Of fish who wear hats and blow silly sails.
They bubble with laughter, splashing our shoes,
As we blissfully dance to our own silly blues.

So next time you wander through nature's sweet fold,
Remember to laugh at the stories retold.
For when the earth whispers, it's pure comedy,
A reminder to cherish our shared harmony!

Twilight's Embrace on the Horizons

Twilight descends with a wink and a smile,
Painting the skies with a whimsical style.
The stars yawn and stretch in their blanket of night,
While fireflies giggle, flashing with delight.

The moon sneaks in with a mischievous grin,
Casting shadows of cats who pretend they're kin.
While crickets conduct a symphony of chirps,
The bunnies hop by, doing jazz with their burps.

As we sip on the breeze, sweet tea in hand,
We ponder life's questions far out of our stand.
With dreams in our pockets and a wink of a star,
We laugh at our follies, wherever they are.

So let twilight's embrace wrap you up tight,
And dance with the shadows who flicker with light.
In this fleeting hour where hilarity plays,
We revel in life's quirky, delightful displays!

Whispers of the Meadow

In the meadow, a bee plays chess,
With a daisy, who's in quite a mess.
They buzz and they laugh, quite the duet,
While the breeze gives them both a wet pet.

A rabbit hops by, wearing a tie,
Says, "Why so serious? Give it a try!"
He flips over a clover, does a quick jig,
While a snail looks on, feeling quite big.

The clouds float above, with quite the view,
A llama in shades yells, "Join the crew!"
The grass tickles toes in a playful way,
As sunbeams shout, "Come out and play!"

All the critters unite to display,
Their silly antics on this fine day.
With giggles and wiggles, they frolic around,
In this patch of joy, pure laughter's found.

Dancing in the Morning Dew

The sun peeks out with a cheeky grin,
A squirrel does ballet, let the fun begin!
The dew drops shimmer, like tiny jewels,
As frogs do the tango, just breaking the rules.

With socks on their ears, the ants strut proud,
While the daisies applaud, cheering out loud.
A plucky old owl gives a hoot and a wink,
Says, "Grab your best moves, don't stop to think!"

The butterflies swirl in a wacky parade,
Spreading confetti from a wild escapade.
They tickle the noses of all that they meet,
As the rooster joins in, tapping his feet.

In this merry scene, laughter's the key,
With everyone joining, not one left to flee.
The spirit of joy dances high and bright,
In the morning dew, everything feels right.

Verdant Echoes

In fields of green, where the goats wear hats,
They chatter about life while ignoring the bats.
A fence post turns sage, with wisdom so grand,
While the geese overhead start a rock band.

Clouds rumble with laughter, quite the surprise,
As the flowers joke back, with twinkling eyes.
The carrots in rows wiggle with glee,
Proud of their stance, as the stars make a spree.

The wind plays a tune on the rustling leaves,
While broccoli claims it's the king of the eves.
With veggie debates rising high in the air,
Each sprout quips a line with comedic flair.

In this lush patch, no moment is dull,
The laughter erupts as each creature may pull.
With echoes of joy that resonate clear,
Nature's own antics, a laugh to endear.

Lullabies of the Prairie

When the stars peek down in the evening glow,
A raccoon croons softly, putting on a show.
The crickets join in, strumming their strings,
As the prairie dogs dance, doing their flings.

Soft whispers of wind add a twist to the tale,
With a purring cat leading the fun without fail.
The owls hoot out rhythms, in perfect time,
Making the night air feel light and sublime.

Fireflies flicker, like notes on a scale,
While the bison, bemused, wag their tails.
A coyote yodels, adding depth to the night,
As all of creation hums lullabies bright.

In this moonlit dance, the laughter runs free,
A joyful serenade, a communal spree.
Under the starlit canopy, dreams take their flight,
With nature's own harmonies, sweet dreams every night.

Gentle Breezes at Twilight

As evening drapes its silent veil,
The crickets start their tiny tale.
With whispers soft, the wind will play,
And tickle grass in a silly way.

The fireflies join in with a dance,
Winking lights in a moonlit trance.
They guide the cows home, somewhat slow,
Mooing thoughts of where they want to go.

Laughter of frogs fills the still air,
Hopping about without a care.
They practice their jokes, an amphibian show,
While a curious cat watches from below.

As twilight claims the golden day,
I chase my hat that's flown away.
With each gust, it flits and sways,
A game of tag in the dusk's embrace.

The Scent of Soft Earth

In springtime's grasp, the soil's alive,
With worms that wiggle, sprout, and thrive.
They plan their own gardening spree,
Sipping the rain with glee, not tea.

The daisies giggle as they bloom,
While clovers plot to find some room.
They throw a party beneath the sun,
With bumblebees buzzing, oh what fun!

A cucumber's wearing a silly hat,
Claiming it's not just a salad brat.
It rolls away, then strikes a pose,
Now that's what I call a garden show!

Amidst the green, I prance and twirl,
Pretending I'm a flower girl.
The breeze laughs at my little jig,
As I trip over a cabbage, oh so big!

Harmony Among Wildflowers

In meadows bright, the colors clash,
Petunias giggle, it's quite the bash.
The sunflowers tower, striking a pose,
While the shy violets blush, nobody knows.

Butterflies flutter with sassy flair,
A fashion show, they just don't care.
Dandelions puff with jokes to share,
Wishing the wind could take them anywhere.

Grasshoppers leap, thinking they're cool,
Conducting an orchestra, who knew in school?
The daisies sway to a tune so sweet,
A symphony only nature could beat.

As laughter blooms where flowers grow,
I skip along, trying to flow.
A bee buzzes by with a fanciful grin,
In this garden of giggles, let the fun begin!

Tidal Serenade of the Fields

The corn stands tall, a golden crew,
Bowing and swaying, just like new.
They hold a concert, rustling loud,
And cheer for the clouds, oh how they proud!

Barley joins with a gentle sway,
While pumpkins practice their ballet.
They giggle as they tumble and roll,
In the chorus of fields, they take control.

The scarecrow's made to laugh with glee,
As crows join in a cacophony.
"Not quite pirates!" he shouts with glee,
"More like clowns at a farmer's jamboree!"

With waves of grain, the rhythm flows,
A dance of joy that only nature knows.
As twilight dims, the stars peek through,
The fields keep singing—how about you?

Memories Woven in Green

In the meadow we danced with glee,
Laughter echoed, wild and free.
A squirrel stole our picnic snack,
We huffed and puffed, but he won't look back.

Sunshine flickered through the leaves,
We played hide-and-seek among the eaves.
A bee buzzed by with a cheeky grin,
'You'll never catch me!' it seemed to spin.

With every step, the grass did sway,
Tickling toes that begged to play.
Memories sweet, like candy coats,
In this place, our laughter floats.

Time may fade, but we'll remain,
Chasing shadows, dancing in the rain.
Oh, how the meadow keeps us young,
In woven memories, forever spun.

Breath of the Ancient Grass

The grass whispers stories old,
Of mischief and dreamers bold.
A frog croaked tales of wobbly hops,
Where the sun wishes the moon never stops.

A cat sneezed loud, interrupting the peace,
Scaring squirrels, making chaos increase.
As wind tickled our noses bright,
We shrieked in joy; oh, what a sight!

Each tuft holds its secrets, so wise,
Unfolding truth in playful guise.
Like a tickle from nature's hand,
Making giggles sprout in this land.

Among the blades, the laughter swells,
As each sneaky breeze tells its spells.
With every rustle, we join the fun,
In the breath of grass, we're forever one.

Silk Threads of Morning Light

Morning dew, a sparkly show,
On blades of green, where giggles grow.
A spider's web with a dazzling flair,
Caught the sun in its silky snare.

A butterfly danced in boisterous spins,
Taunting the ants with their tiny bins.
They grumbled and gritched, plotting a race,
While daisies chuckled at their haste.

The wind played tricks, gave us a start,
Whisking our hats like an agile dart.
We tumbled and rolled, with glee so bright,
In this quilt of dreams, we took flight.

Silk threads spun in the morning's kiss,
Each moment, a giggle, a sweet, silly bliss.
Together we twirled, with joy in our hearts,
Finding light in laughter, where nonsense starts.

Songs of the Meadowland

In the meadow, the grass sings loud,
Each blade a note in a playful crowd.
Grasshoppers joined with a rhyming beat,
Creating a symphony, oh what a treat!

The daisies swayed like pops in a row,
Dancing to the tune of a breezy show.
While a wandering squirrel joined in the fun,
Twirling around, thinking it's number one.

A chorus of frogs croaked out their lines,
While crickets strummed their tiny shrines.
Laughter and music filled the air,
This meadowland magic, beyond compare.

As we joined the song in our wild parade,
The sun painted laughter, a bright cascade.
With arms outstretched to the skies so grand,
We danced and sang in this meadowland.

Connecting to the Roots

In a field where laughter grows,
Roots twist like a dance with toes.
Worms wiggle in their funky gear,
Garden gnomes give a hearty cheer.

Bees buzz with a silly grin,
Chasing flowers, they spin and spin.
Frogs croak out their best dad jokes,
While butterflies flap, playing puns with folks.

The soil's secrets we dig up with glee,
Digging deeper, what will we see?
A potato wearing a tiny hat,
Is it food, or did we just find a cat?

With shovels and rakes, we laugh and play,
Creating mischief, come what may.
Connecting to roots, our joy's a blast,
In this garden where giggles are cast.

Sunlit Journeys in the Meadow

In the meadow where daisies shout,
Sunbeams dance, there's no doubt.
Grass tickles toes as we run wild,
Chasing butterflies like a playful child.

Squirrels are plotting a nutty race,
While rabbits hop with perfect grace.
A picnic spread with sandwiches stacked,
But ants are quick; they've already attacked!

With every step, mischief can bloom,
Sunlit joy fills the air with a boom.
We strike poses like silly statues,
As the wind joins in with its laughter too.

When the sun dips low, we wave goodbye,
And back to our homes, we will fly.
Across the meadow, with giggles in tow,
Sunlit journeys, a joyous show.

Fragments of Earth's Breath

Feel the whispers of the ground,
In every corner, laughter is found.
The trees chuckle in the gentle breeze,
As squirrels hold conferences with ease.

The daisies compete in a funny hat show,
With petals unfolding in a comical flow.
A bumblebee pulls off a graceful flip,
Spilling nectar from its hefty trip.

In puddles where frogs play leapfrog cheer,
Their chorus of croaks is the music we hear.
A turtle competes in a speed race with snails,
While the sun winks on as laughter prevails.

Fragments of nature's whimsical breath,
Merging giggles with a touch of depth.
In every patch of wild, there's room for glee,
Where earth's funny heart beats endlessly.

Harmonies of the Homestead

At the homestead, where the funny things grow,
Chickens sing solos in a clucking show.
The porch swings sway, telling tales untold,
As Grandpa's stories never get old.

A cat in a hat, oh what a sight!
Chasing shadows in the morning light.
On the fence, goats strike a pose supreme,
Join in the jam, it's a barnyard dream!

Fireside tales with marshmallows in hand,
Roasting s'mores on the smoothy sand.
The stars wink down, joining the fun,
In the homestead, it's a whimsical run.

With laughter and warmth as our guide,
We dance under stars, side by side.
The harmonies echo, sweet and clear,
In our cozy homestead, joy is near.

Caress of the Verdant

In fields so bright, green blades do sway,
   They tickle feet on a sunny day.
I dance and prance with a wild delight,
   Laughing at bugs that take to flight.

The grass, it whispers secrets bold,
Of squirrels plotting—oh, the stories told!
   I trip and fall, I roll down hills,
While nature giggles, then calls for thrills.

In the breeze, the flowers tease,
A game of tag with buzzing bees.
   Around I spin, a dizzy joy,
Join me, oh dear, my playful boy!

The verdant world has such a flair,
With pranks hidden just everywhere.
So let's rejoice in nature's charm,
And find the grass that smells like calm.

Ballad of the Wildflowers

Wildflowers laugh as they bloom away,
Dancing in sun, come what may.
Petals wear colors like rainbow beads,
Shaking their hips in the summer reeds.

A daisy winks, a tulip sighs,
The garden's a circus with all its highs.
Bees in tuxedos, butterflies too,
All join the show with a grand debut.

I feign to pluck a flower near,
But get whacked by a thistle—oh dear!
The wildflowers giggle, they've had their fun,
As I retreat, shouting, "Let's run!"

With laughter echoing through the field,
To this floral army, I gladly yield.
Their beauty fierce, their humor spry,
In a world of blooms, I can't deny!

Chasing Shadows in the Pastures

In the pasture, shadows skip and twirl,
Chasing the sun with a cheeky whirl.
A cow gives chase, with a moooo as a cue,
While goats stargaze at the bright sky blue.

A shadow races; I dart in tow,
It ducks, it weaves, oh where did it go?
The sheep start bleating like they're on cue,
"Join the chase! We're following too!"

Beneath the trees, the fun takes flight,
Where squirrels plot more mischief tonight.
I laugh out loud, the day's quite a treat,
With dancing shadows and furry feet.

As night creeps in, we bow to the moon,
The pasture feels full, a jazzy tune.
These antics with shadows, so grand in sight,
In laughter and light, we bid goodnight!

A Symphony of Green

Winged serenaders sing through the trees,
While frogs croak along with the summer breeze.
A symphony blooms in hues of delight,
As laughter echoes through day and night.

The grass plays piano under my toes,
While dandelions sway with each little pose.
A chorus of critters joins in the fun,
Their quirky tunes shine bright as the sun.

I'm drawing circles 'round ants on parade,
While they dutifully march, a sly charade.
The ants whisper songs of a tasty crumb,
While I cavort here, lost in the hum.

In this orchestra, life sounds so bright,
With earthy rhythms and sheer delight.
So join the dance, let the music flow,
In the symphony green, we steal the show.

The Promise of Growth

In fields where dreams of green are sown,
Tiny shoots push through the stone.
They dance and sway in breezy cheer,
While squirrels hold debates, oh so near.

The daisies giggle in the sun,
Complaining, 'Why can't we have some fun?'
In the shade, the mushrooms plot,
A cap-tivating scheme that they have got.

Ants march on with snacks galore,
But one forgot the restroom door!
A fight ensues, a very funny sight,
While butterflies just take flight.

So here we cheer for growth so spry,
With laughter echoing in the sky.
In nature's arms, we find delight,
As seeds of joy take their flight.

Wandering Through the Wildflowers

Upon a hill where wild blooms sing,
I met a bee with quite the sting.
He buzzed around, so full of pride,
'This pollen's mine—just step aside!'

The daisies whispered secrets sweet,
While clovers played hide and seek at my feet.
A dandelion took a daring leap,
'We're all weeds, but we're fun to keep!'

A ladybug with polka dots bright,
Told tales of her daring flight.
While butterflies approach with flair,
'You've got something stuck in your hair!'

Laughter blooms in every petal,
In this garden, joy's the metal.
So come along, take a dive,
With wildflowers, we're all alive!

Interlacing Paths of Green

On winding paths where green things roam,
Lions of grass declare their home.
While hedgehogs wear their prickly hats,
In wild parades, just like diplomat chitchats.

I saw a snail move quite so slow,
Saying, 'I've got all week, you know!'
While worms played chess beneath the mud,
But forgot the rules, oh what a dud!

The trees all swayed with playful ease,
While insects threw a massive tease.
'Look at us!' they proudly buzzed,
And ants just sighed, 'Oh please, we're fuzzed!'

In tangled vines we weave our tale,
With laughter sown like every trail.
So roam the green and join the cheer,
In nature's play, we have no fear.

Echoes of Elation

In morning's hug and sunshine's grin,
The flowers whisper, 'Let's begin!'
With comical crows doing their dance,
'We're cool birds too, just take a chance!'

The echoes of a chuckle float,
As butterflies wear a party coat.
A fox with flair, who acts a clown,
Calls for all to come to town!

The daisies formed a quirky band,
With marigolds, they've made a stand.
But when the ants stole all the shoes,
They turned the show into a snooze!

So here's to all the merry mirth,
In every laugh, we find our worth.
With echoes ringing through the land,
Join nature's laughter, hand in hand.

Mother Earth's Gentle Caress

In a patch of green, I found my shoes,
They played hide and seek with the morning dew.
A squirrel grinned, stole my tasty snack,
While I just stared, wondering what I lack.

The sun wore shades, a floppy hat too,
This planet sways like it's in a zoo.
The flowers giggle, tickled by the breeze,
Even the ants march, strutting with such ease.

Caterpillars dance on cabbage's head,
While lucky worms get to lie in bed.
A breeze whispers jokes, I can't quite hear,
But I can tell, they're all about cheer.

With nature's wit, life finds a way,
Turning the mundane into a play.
So grab your hat, let's skip and prance,
In Mother Earth's gentle, silly dance.

Tides of Time in Bloom

The clock ticks loud on this sunny shore,
Seagulls squawk like they're wanting more.
Each wave's a laugh, splashing on the sand,
Time's a jokester with a silly hand.

Seashells whisper secrets, tales so tall,
Of underwater parties in a coral hall.
Crabs in tuxedos, dancing in style,
Making us chuckle with their clever guile.

The horizon giggles, a bright orange glow,
While flip-flops trip and tumble, oh no!
Sandcastles crumble, but who really cares?
Every grain feels like it's part of our fares.

So let the tides giggle and ebb away,
Life's a beach party, come what may.
With waves of laughter, we'll dance in bloom,
Savoring moments that light up the room.

The Language of Leaf and Stem

Leaves talk gossip when the wind is near,
As branches nod, lending an eager ear.
The flowers blush in their vibrant hues,
Sharing spicy tales of the morning dews.

Roots dig deep, in a silent debate,
While buds tease blooms, 'Can you find the fate?'
Bumblebees buzz with a goofy hum,
Planting each joke, making sure it's fun.

The trees are comedians, stand-up in the park,
With bark that's rough and humor that's stark.
Each leaf a letter, each stem a rhyme,
In nature's play, we're lost in time.

So gather around where the laughter's seen,
In this language of green, we share and glean.
With every giggle, every chuckle, and cheer,
Nature's amusing, it's perfectly clear.

Patches of Sun and Shade

Under the sun, my hat starts to fry,
While shade's a cool whisper, a soothing sigh.
The daisies yawn while popping out their heads,
While crickets make bets on who sleeps in beds.

A butterfly flits, a colorful tease,
Announcing the jokes from the buzzing bees.
Patches of laughter, bright spots of glee,
Nature's a comedian, just wait and see.

In the dappled light, shadows dance with delight,
As squirrels make puns that are quite out of sight.
The breeze is a bard, strumming leaves like strings,
Creating sweet melodies that tickle our wings.

So come take a seat in this humorous glade,
Where every chuckle casts worries away.
Let's giggle together in sun and shade,
In this patchy wonderland, joyfully made.

Weaving Dreams in the Fields

In fields of green where dreams are spun,
The earth laughs hard, it's all in fun.
With tangled thoughts like strands of hay,
We weave our wishes, come what may.

A horse named Gus just wants a snack,
He'll steal your hat, but not your back.
We chase him round, it's quite a sight,
His attitude? A pure delight.

The daisies dance to nature's beat,
While bunnies hop on tiny feet.
With every stitch, a giggle grows,
As sunshine warms the silly toes.

Our dreams take flight like butterflies,
In colorful hues beneath the skies.
With laughter and a dash of cheer,
We weave our lives, year after year.

An Invitation to the Stillness

Come sit with me beneath the tree,
Let's sip some tea and count the bees.
The breeze will whisper silly tales,
Of clumsy ants and dancing snails.

The squirrel poses, oh so spry,
With acorn hat, he waves goodbye.
While shadows play a game of tag,
My thoughts run wild, they dance and brag.

Invitations sealed with dandelion fluff,
To join a party—oh, wasn't that tough!
We'll sing the songs of nature's choir,
And twirl about till we retire.

So breathe in deep the fragrant air,
Let's catch our giggles everywhere.
In stillness, find the jests that bloom,
Together, laugh away the gloom.

Fragrant Whispers of the Earth

Whispers flow on winds so sweet,
With scents of flowers at our feet.
A farting bee makes quite a sound,
As sticky nectar rolls around.

The herbs are prone to mischief too,
With parsley plotting just for you.
A sprinkle here, a dash of that,
In gardens where the gnomes just chat.

Mushrooms giggle in the shade,
With polka dots in their parade.
And daisies wink at every passerby,
Their secrets shared with a cheeky sigh.

The earth will chuckle, bold and bright,
With every twist of nature's light.
So gather round, you merry folk,
And share a laugh—the best kind of joke!

Cultivating the Quiet

We plant our thoughts in rows so neat,
In quiet corners where stillness meets.
The weeds are dancing, oh my word,
While rabbits plot—yeah, haven't you heard?

We cultivate our joy with care,
Yet daisies grow without a fare.
With trowels raised, we dig and laugh,
At muddy shoes—our own path's staff.

The sun sets slow, a golden hue,
While fireflies join our merry crew.
We sip on lemonade, oh-so-sweet,
As crickets serenade our beat.

Embracing calm amidst the play,
In fields where gentle whispers sway.
Each chuckle echoes through the night,
In cultivated quiet, pure delight.

A Stroll Through Nature's Heart

In fields where daisies play peek-a-boo,
Grass tickles toes as we wander through.
A squirrel tries to steal my sandwich slice,
But I laugh, he's got a knack for being nice.

The trees nod along to our silly song,
While birds chirp out a tune all day long.
A rabbit hops by with a comical flair,
And the whole forest chuckles in the warm air.

Sunshine dances on the rippling creek,
Frogs in a chorus, oh, what a cheek!
We wave to the ants in their busy parade,
Nature's laughter is never delayed.

So let's twirl and jig beneath the vast sky,
With flowers as crowns, we'll surely fly high.
In this charming realm where whimsy is free,
Every step is a giggle, just you and me.

Breaths of the Brisk Breeze

The wind tickles my nose; what a surprise!
It whispers secrets, it giggles and flies.
I try to catch it; oh, what a chase!
It swirls round my head, sets a laugh on my face.

Pine trees sway in a dandy dance,
While butterflies flutter in a breezy prance.
Clouds look like pillows floating so high,
As I chuckle and wave at the laughing sky.

On a picnic rug, sandwiches stacked,
A mischievous raccoon has my snack attacked.
I shout, 'Hey, buddy! Did you forget?
You can't just take it—there's crumbs, you bet!'

Still, nature's humor is hard to withstand,
With giggling flowers waving their hand.
So let's breathe in this brisk and bright air,
Life's funny moments are everywhere!

Whispers of the Meadow

In the meadow where daisies chat,
A cow wanders in, quite round and fat.
"Hey there, friend!" I jest with a wink,
She beams back at me, or so I think.

Butterflies flutter like tiny balloons,
Their colors burst out to the light of the moon.
A grasshopper chirps with a rhythm so tight,
As we all join the dance in the soft twilight.

The breeze brings tales of joy and glee,
Even the mushrooms share laughter with me.
Glancing about, see the ants in a row,
Marching to music they only can know.

So let's sip on sunshine and giggle aloud,
In nature's embrace, we're blissfully proud.
Here in the meadow, life's full of delight,
With whispers of laughter that last through the night.

The Fragrance of Dawn

As dawn breaks in a blush of gold,
The flowers unfurl, stories unfold.
A hummingbird zooms, silly as can be,
Buzzing around like it's lost in a spree.

The morning mist tickles my feet,
While grasshoppers hop to the rhythm so sweet.
"Good morning!" I cheer to the sun up high,
It winks at me, as it begins to fly.

With pancakes in hand, I scout for a place,
To laugh with the critters in a friendly race.
A playful fox darts, a flash of red,
As if whispering, "Join me; let's hit the spread!"

In this fragrant dawn where joy reigns supreme,
Every moment feels like a vibrant dream.
So let's soak it in, this delightful show,
With nature's perfume, oh, how we'll glow!

Visions of a Sunlit Field

In a field where daisies dance with glee,
A cow snags the leash of a bee.
The sun shines bright, the sky so blue,
While squirrels debate who made the best stew.

The rabbits hop with a comedic flair,
Chasing their shadows without a care.
A chicken clucks jokes that go over my head,
While the fox takes notes, then steals all the bread.

A pair of goats argue over a shoe,
Claiming it's fashion, oh who knew?
The day rolls on, laughter rings free,
While critters all joke, "Life's all about tea!"

Under skies where laughter's spun,
The field awakens with bursts of fun.
Nature's circus, where whimsy abounds,
In every giggle, joy resounds.

Tending to the Spiral of Life

In the garden, where weeds like to scoff,
A snail races slowly, then trips and rolls off.
Cacti wear costumes, oh what a sight,
While daisies make crowns, feeling quite bright.

A squirrel's a florist, with acorns in tow,
The flowers giggle, take things super slow.
The worms throw a dance party beneath the earth,
Celebrating soil, oh what a rebirth!

Pruning the laughter, trimming the hue,
Spinning vines twirl while the daisies accrue.
With each little chuckle that nature imparts,
Our world's made of joy and of colorful hearts.

So tend to your garden, let silliness bloom,
Joy thrives in the light, dispelling all gloom.
In this spiral of life, where fun's never rife,
We'll dance with the weeds, celebrating our strife.

Threads of Nature's Embrace

Woven like stories, the branches all sway,
Whispering secrets of kids who play.
A dandelion sneezes—what a surprise!
Pollen coats bees like confetti in skies.

The sun's a jester, tickling the leaves,
While ants march along—"We're hard at our leaves!"
Spiders spin webs that gleam in bright light,
A butterfly giggles, "They're giving me fright!"

The wind plays tricks, blowing hats off the heads,
A turkey struts by in bright purple threads.
With every twist, nature's laughter runs wild,
Even the clouds join, like a playful child.

So dance with the breezes, let laughter take flight,
In threads of the world, find joy in the light.
Embrace every moment, from early to late,
For nature's a quilt, sewn with playful fate.

The Sigh of the Earth

The earth lets out sighs, more like a big laugh,
When daisies wiggle and play, it's a gaffe.
A frog jumps for joy, a splash marks the score,
While ants hold debates on who's winning the war.

A crow tells a joke, pecking crumbs on the road,
While the beetles all scatter—"Oh no! Here's the load!"
The puddles reflect all the playful distress,
And the sun rolls its eyes, finding it a mess.

With humor in roots and mirth in the sky,
The earth hums a tune that's sweet as cherry pie.
Every chuckle of nature, a riddle to cheer,
Let's dance with the flora, we'll all disappear!

So breathe in the laughter, let chuckles unfold,
In the sigh of the earth, life's funny and bold.
A world spun in joy, with whimsy always near,
Let's celebrate nature, for laughter we steer.

Embrace of Nature's Tapestry

In the garden, worms do dance,
They wiggle in their muddy pants.
Bees play tag with butterflies,
As daisies wear their sunny ties.

A squirrel steals a picnic crumb,
While robins sing in goofy hum.
The trees gossip like friends in tea,
Nature's circus, come see, come see!

Ants march by in tidy rows,
Forming lines like tiny shows.
With every step, they joke and prance,
As if they've all won a dance chance!

The sun pops up with a grin so wide,
While shadows play hide and seek outside.
Nature's laughter fills the air,
A whimsical world, oh, do you dare?

A Chorus of Sunlit Days

Clouds wear capes like snoopy gnomes,
Playing tricks with sunlit homes.
Winds play tunes on leaves' soft backs,
The sun beams down on grassy knacks.

Beetles roll like little balls,
And flowers giggle, make silly calls.
The sun is bright, the day is sweet,
As nature dances on happy feet!

Frogs croak jokes beneath the moon,
While fireflies blink in a funny tune.
The night brings laughter, the stars agree,
In this joyous, wild jubilee!

Breezes blow in playful swirls,
Tickling fur of dancing squirrels.
The world's a stage, a laugh parade,
Join in the fun, don't be afraid!

The Rhythm of Wild Blossoms

Flowers twist in breezy cheer,
Doing the cha-cha, aren't they dear?
Bees in bowties, buzzing proud,
Join in the dance, sing out loud!

Dandelions spread their seeds,
In tiny puffs, they plant their needs.
With giggles, petals take a spin,
In nature's show, let fun begin!

A ladybug plays peek-a-boo,
With butterflies in skies so blue.
While daisies wear their polka dots,
Each bloom shares secrets, oh, lots and lots!

As the sun sets, laughter glows,
Crickets chirp their silly shows.
The night wraps up this playful spree,
In wild blossoms, come dance with me!

Celestial Ribbons of Dawn

Morning breaks with a giggle bright,
As shadows scamper, what a sight!
The sky paints smiles in shades of pink,
While sleepy things begin to blink.

The sun stretches, yawns, and beams,
Tickling clouds from their dreamy dreams.
A rooster shouts, "Time to get up!"
While coffee cups spill the morning cup!

Rabbits hop in their fluffy shoes,
Chasing each other, giggling, too.
The flowers wake, and dance in play,
Painting the dawn in a bright bouquet!

As day unfolds with whimsy and fun,
Each moment shines, we've just begun.
Embrace this cheer, let laughter soar,
For nature's tales are forever more!

Echoes of Nature's Heart

In the woods, squirrels debate,
Who will steal the last treat?
The raccoon just laughs at their fate,
As he feasts on crumbs so sweet.

The birds gossip high in the trees,
About the bee who can't dance.
They flutter and flap in the breeze,
While the bumblebee takes a chance.

A squirrel in shades by the stream,
Claims he's the king of the park.
He digs through the soil, a wild dream,
But ends up just finding a lark.

Beneath the moon's playful glare,
A band of fireflies prance wide.
They light up the night with flair,
While frogs just watch and abide.

Beneath the Canopy

Under leaves, the shadows play,
A rabbit hops in quick delight.
He stops to munch, then skitters away,
From a turtle that moves with might.

The chipmunks have formed a parade,
Marching around like tiny ants.
But one gets lost, his plans delayed,
And now he's in a plant trance.

A wise owl hoots with a grin,
Awake when others are not.
He hoards all the gossip and sin,
While dreaming of the next plot.

But beneath this wooden retreat,
Life's hilarity knows no bounds.
Fungi dance, and roots have a seat,
As laughter in nature resounds.

Lullabies of the Prairie

In fields where the daisies dare,
A cow sings off-key with flair.
Her friends stampede but she won't care,
For reasons, she can't seem to share.

The wind whispers secrets untold,
To the grasses that sway and spin.
They giggle and whisper of old,
While the cactus just rolls its grin.

A coyote howls just for show,
Though it's offbeat, he won't give in.
His echo leaves the prairie aglow,
While the rabbits just laugh with a spin.

Under stars, the crickets strum,
They dream of a tune that won't quit.
Yet harmony's lost in the hum,
As nature joins in with a wit.

Threads of Earth's Bounty

In gardens where the veggies sprout,
Tomatoes wiggle, full of cheer.
They giggle, they squirm, there's no doubt,
As peppers plot from their rear.

Zucchini stretches with glee,
While radishes play hide and seek.
But the lettuce is far too free,
Waving like it's the last week.

Bees buzz in a rhythm so sweet,
Doing dances that make us grin.
They're off to find the finest treat,
While the daisies are taking a spin.

With threads of color, life's mapped out,
In the dirt, there's laughter and mirth.
From the earth to the skies, it's about,
The whimsical joy of true worth.

Breathing Life into the Fields

In the fields where the breeze likes to play,
Cows dance in circles, come join their ballet.
With hats made of hay, they twirl with delight,
Under the sun's giggles, oh what a sight!

The farmer's hat flies, caught in a gust,
He chases it down, it's a comedy bust!
Chickens now plotting their feathery flair,
Dreaming of crowns, but they can't style hair.

As daisies gossip and the tulips tease,
The weeds throw a party, come join if you please!
With laughter and pollen, they dance in a clump,
Jumping and jiving, now rapping like thump!

So come take a stroll in this whimsical patch,
Where everything giggles and nothing's a catch.
Fields filled with laughter, a botanical cheer,
Life's little circus, and the big top is near!

Ode to the Wind's Caress

Oh wind, dear wind, with a tickle and tease,
You steal all my hats like it's one of your wheezes.
You swirl and you twirl, a mischievous sprite,
Playing pranks on the trees, what a glorious sight!

You kiss all the flowers, make petals whirl round,
But don't blame the bees when they bump on the ground!

They buzz and they fumble, like they've had too much drink,
Thanks to your zephyr, they're more tipsy than you think!

You squeeze through the cracks in the old garden gate,
Whispering secrets, it must be so great!
But please, dear wind, do be careful, I implore,
Don't carry my pants just like you did before!

So here's to your breezes, so charming, yet wild,
The sweet gusts, the howlers, every last child.
We're all in your hands, like balloons in the air,
Don't let go too sudden, oh please, if you care!

Beneath the Open Sky

Under the vastness, where the odd clouds float,
I met a lone pigeon, who fancied a coat.
He waddled and strutted, with style quite bizarre,
But he wore it with pride, our runway superstar!

Sunshine pours down like it's trying to bake,
My ice cream is melting, oh what a mistake!
The ants come to gather, they've got a plan,
To launch a sweet heist, how clever they ran!

The grass whispers secrets of all things absurd,
While the squirrels debate over nuts they've secured.
A turtle shared gossip on who's fastest in town,
But we're all just slow folks, losing our frown.

So let's lie back, count the clouds in their flight,
And laugh at the antics that bring us delight.
For beneath this grand sky, life's simply a show,
With every odd character putting on a glow!

Where Silence Meets the Bloom

In the garden's embrace, where plants like to chat,
The daisies are dreaming of being a cat.
They'd swish 'round all day, in their flowery grace,
While the roses roll eyes, lost in their lace.

A quiet debate, held 'neath whispering leaves,
About who has perfume that truly deceives.
The lilies all giggle, a fragrant affair,
As the bees form a buzz band, pulling in air.

In this quiet bloom, laughter hides in the shade,
While the violets squabble over beauty displayed.
A fluffy old bunny just dreaming of fun,
Thinks he's the gardener, making flowers run!

So here in the silence, they blossom and muse,
With each little petal, new tales to amuse.
And though we may ponder their secrets unseen,
This garden of laughter is fit for a queen!

A Tapestry of Blades

The lawnmower revved, a symphony in blue,
With blades that dance like a jazz band crew.
Grass flies high, like confetti in the air,
While squirrels applaud from their branchy chair.

The weeds revolt, they're plotting a coup,
In the garden's shadows, they're brewing a stew.
But here comes the hose, with a squirt and a spray,
"Not today, my friends, I'm the hero of the day!"

The flowers giggle, they sway with delight,
As bugs do a jig in the warm sunlight.
The garden's alive, with laughter and cheer,
Even the gnomes are cracking a beer!

So here's to the blades, the comrades of glee,
They cut through the chaos, they keep us carefree.
In the tapestry of life, we weave a bright shade,
Where humor and grass have merrily played.

Serenade Under the Sky

At twilight's hush, the stars blink in tune,
A raccoon croons softly to the light of the moon.
"Join me, dear fireflies," it seems to plead,
"We'll dance till the night's lost in stardust seed."

The crickets compose an orchestra grand,
With violins made of twigs in each hand.
They harmonize right with a cacophony of fun,
While the owls hoot in a gravity-free run!

The breeze whispers jokes that the daisies can tell,
As they chuckle and twirl in their flowery shell.
"Why did the garden feel so spry?"
"Because it had roots in laughter — oh, my!"

So let's serenade until morning's first blush,
With critters and blooms, a glorious hush.
A concert of chaos, a melody blessed,
Who knew that nature could make us so jest?

Morning's Velvet Embrace

The sun peeks up like an eager old friend,
Giving a wink, "Let the mischief transcend!"
Birds find their voices, a cacophony bright,
As they chirp silly tales in the morning light.

The toast pops up in a joyful surprise,
While coffee grumbles with dreams in its eyes.
The milk's doing ballet, the sugar's a star,
As breakfast becomes a wild breakfast bazaar!

So step into dawn with a skip and a hum,
Where pancakes sing songs about syrup's great sum.
The table laughs loud with dishes aglow,
"Eat up, dear friend, let the good times flow!"

With giggles and grins in this dawn's sweet embrace,
The morning unfolds at a whimsical pace.
In the heart of the kitchen, love stirs and grates,
A symphony mixed with delicious debates.

The Dance of Green

In a leafy ballroom where grasses sway,
The daisies are twirling in a whimsical fray.
Sunflowers spin, on their tall wooden shoes,
While clover kids giggle, spreading good news.

The ants in their suits march in perfect formation,
Arranging a flash mob in joyous elation.
"Hey, caterpillar, join the shimmy and slide!
The fun's too good, do not hide inside!"

A ladybug leads with a flick of her wings,
As the whole garden bursts into laughter and sings.
"Let's salsa with shadows and pirouette sprout,
In this dance of the green, there's joy all about!"

So come join the frolic, where nature's the queen,
With each giggle shared, life's an evergreen scene.
In this verdant jubilee, let your worries unfurl,
And dance with the plants in a blissful whirl!

Dances in the Dappled Sun

The grass does sway, it tickles my toes,
While squirrels prance, striking epic poses.
A jig with the daisies, who knew they could dance?
Twirl with the breeze, we'll take a chance.

Sunlight winks, caught in a giggle,
As I trip over roots, my feet start to wiggle.
Bees buzzing tunes, a slapstick ballet,
Nature's comedy shows, come out to play.

Beneath the trees, shadows throw a party,
With crickets chirping, their rhythm is hearty.
Mushrooms pop up, just to join in the fun,
An all-species fest, with no need to run.

So let's prance through the glades, full of cheer,
With laughter and blossoms, the world feels so dear.
Amidst all the chaos, a wild, sweet refrain:
Life's just a laugh, remember the gain.

Embracing the Horizon

A bird on a branch is sharing a joke,
While clouds debate if they're puff or smoke.
The horizon stretches, a cartoonish smile,
Waving to travelers across every mile.

Mountains wear hats, snow-capped and grand,
As the river whispers its top-secret plan.
Cacti wear sunglasses, too cool to show,
In this humorous vista where giggles can grow.

Skies paint a canvas of jellybean hues,
While butterflies flutter in dapper shoes.
Embracing the day with light-hearted glee,
Each step feels like laughter; come dance with me!

So let's wander onward, with mischief to spare,
With horizons embracing, and nothing but air.
For life, in its splendor, asks us to grin,
Adventure awaits; let's just dive right in!

The Language of the Soil

In the world of the dirt, worms throw a parade,
They wiggle and giggle, no need for charades.
With compost confetti, they do a cha-cha,
Making the ground sing with a wild hoorah!

Mole plots a racket, a burrowing champ,
While roots tell secrets beside the old lamp.
They whisper of rain, of sunshine, and dirt,
A banquet of chatter in each leafy skirt.

A garden of humor, where laughter takes root,
With marigolds blushing, in bloom — oh so cute!
With each little sprout, a punchline's unfurled,
A ticklish embrace of the muckiest world.

So let's dig with joy in our hands, never shy,
With a mantra of giggles beneath the wide sky.
For in this rich dance of the soil and the sun,
Life's hearty humor is never outdone!

Echoing the Wild

In the forest, the trees are chitchatting loud,
Their leaves rustle secrets, a gossiping crowd.
While squirrels debate, who's the best acrobat,
The echoing wild is a playful habitat.

Foxes in bowties sneak up for a peek,
Hiding in bushes, they plot and they sneak.
With bears in pajamas, lounging so tight,
Every creature a comedian, what a wild sight!

The river rejoices and splashes in glee,
As otters perform, making waves of a spree.
With rhythm and laughter, they play by the brook,
In this lively scene, all are off the hook.

So let's follow the giggles, the whispers of cheer,
In the echoing wild, every moment is clear.
A symphony of jesters, a nature-filled fond,
In this comedy of life, we all share the bond!

Dreams in the Breeze

A dancing hairpin, lost on a dare,
A whisper of breeze, tickling my hair.
I chase after winks from the clouds up high,
While grasshoppers giggle, as I stumble by.

I dreamed I could fly, with a kite in my hand,
But tangled in ribbons, I just couldn't stand.
The sky is my canvas, my hopes take a flight,
But laughter erupts when I'm stuck in mid-flight.

The wind takes a turn, my dreams spin and flip,
Like marbles on pavement, they all start to slip.
But amidst all the chaos, a smile breaks through,
It's fun to be foolish, who knew it was true?

So I'll leap with abandon, and dance with the trees,
Life's knot may be tight, but I'll still feel the breeze.
With laughter as music, and joy at my side,
In dreams of the air, I will forever glide.

Harmony in the Meadow

In the meadow, cows moo a sweet serenade,
While frogs in full chorus invoke their charade.
The daisies are nodding, the bees find their beat,
A concert of nature, oh, nothing's more sweet!

The butterflies flutter, doing the cha-cha,
While ants march in line, singing their own opera.
The sun wears a smile, as the breeze starts to dance,
And daisies sway gently in a carefree trance.

A rabbit hops in, tapping a toe,
To the rhythm of laughter, their spirits aglow.
The laughter of daisies, a whimsical sight,
In this meadow of humor, everything's bright.

So come join the party, lay down on the grass,
With giggles and wiggles, let time simply pass.
In harmony's embrace, let the foolishness reign,
For in every chuckle, there's pleasure again!

The Grass That Sings

Once I heard the grass sing, oh, what a delight,
It crooned silly tunes on a starry night.
The crickets joined in, with a tap-tap-tap,
While fireflies danced in a sparkly flap.

The daisies chimed in, harmonious and bright,
With a doo-wop refrain, they brought sheer delight.
The winds played the trumpet, the clouds sang the bass,
In this meadow of music, there's always a space.

Then came a great tumble, I tripped on a tune,
Landed right in a patch, beneath a full moon.
The grass roared with laughter, as the night wore on,
In a concert of giggles, till the crack of the dawn.

So when you hear nature hum, stop for a while,
Join the rhythm of life, let your spirit smile.
In the dance of the grass, there's magic to cling,
Where every note played is a reason to sing.

Twilight's Gentle Touch

In twilight's embrace, as the day starts to frown,
The fireflies emerge with their own little crown.
They flicker like stars, take a flight with great glee,
Winking at me, saying, "Come, join the spree!"

The moon's a round cookie, just pulled from the oven,
It glows in the night, while the crickets are lovin'.
They chirp silly lyrics, with laughter so sweet,
As I trip on the grass, and land on my feet!

There's a breeze weaving stories, of nonsense and cheer,
With whispers of sunbeams that drifted quite near.
The shadows are giggling, they play hide and seek,
While I twirl like a dancer, feeling carefree and meek.

So here in this moment, as the sun bids goodbye,
I'll savor the softness of twilight's sly sigh.
With chuckles and winks, I'll embrace what it brings,
For you never outgrow the joy that it sings!

www.ingramcontent.com/pod-product-compliance
Lightning Source LLC
Chambersburg PA
CBHW051640160426
43209CB00004B/728